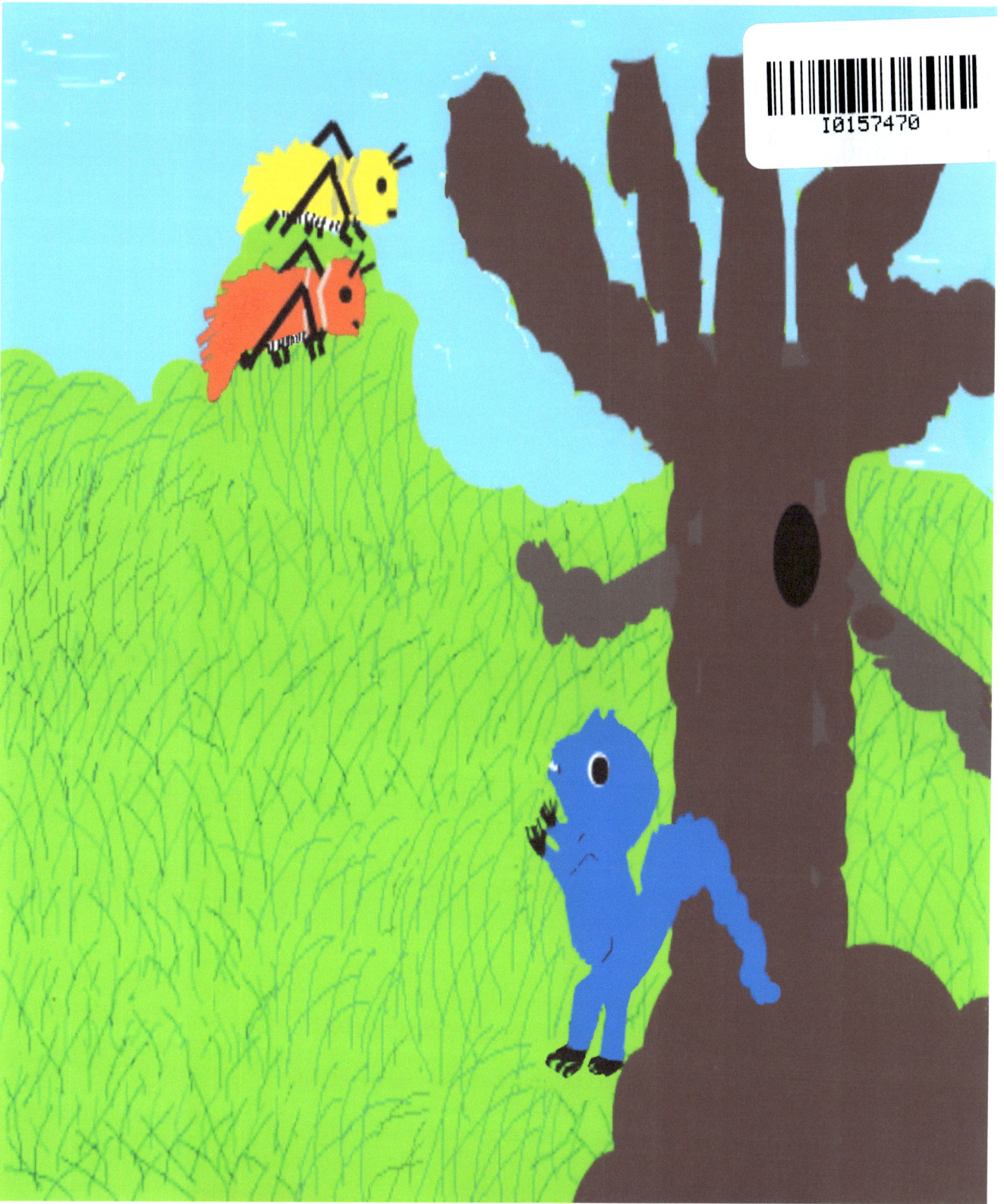

Koo, Moo, and Mr. Squirrel

Written and illustrated by Elizabeth B. Onabajo (LizB)

Independently Published

ISBN 978-1-0687516-0-8

First published in the UK on Tuesday, November 5, 2024

A catalogue record for this book is available from the British Library.

Dedication

For All Children

Introduction

Koo and Moo hop and skip. They make music and sing.

Druzzzzz-xixxxxx-druzzzzz! Xixxxxx-druzzzzz-xixxxxx.

They do not want to teach Mr. Squirrel how to make music.

Guess why Koo and Moo do not want to teach

Mr. Squirrel how to make music?

Mr. Squirrel is a little bit sad.

Afterwards, he makes his own music.

He sings, and he is happy. He also makes other squirrels happy.

Grasshoppers are good hoppers, but can they sing?

What about squirrels?

Koo and Moo are two little grasshoppers.

They are twin brother and twin sister.

They are good at skipping and hopping.

Koo and Moo's mother let them out to skip and hop.

They skip and hop on the green grass.

Mother is not skipping with Koo and Moo for a good reason.

She wants to prepare supper.

She skips skipping to collect food-stuff from the skip.

She is so fast, she always skips chatting to the farmer.

The farmer owns the skip.

He allows the mother grasshopper

to collect vegetables and seeds from the skip.

He uses them to make compost to grow more vegetables and fruits.

Koo and Moo's mother hops in and out of the farmer's skip. She collects the best vegetables and seeds for supper. She always skips being seen by the chicken.
After skipping, Koo and Moo will have some food to eat.

They never skip their meals.

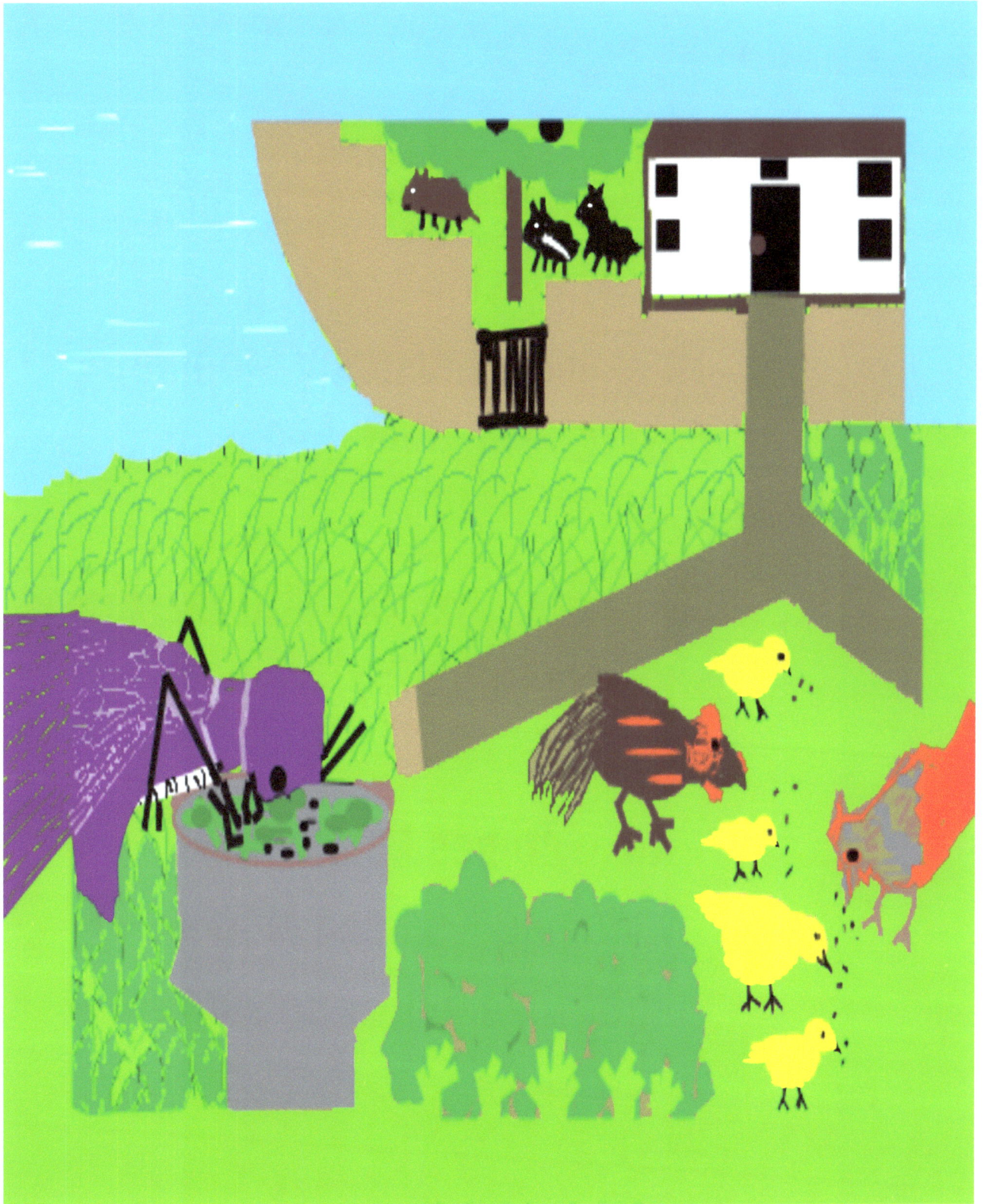

Koo and Moo make music.
They skip and hop.
They make music by tapping
their legs against their wings.

Druzzzzz-Xixxxxx-druzzzzz!
Xixxxxx-druzzzzz-xixxxxx.

Next, comes Mr. Squirrel,
watching Koo and Moo as
they skip, hop, and sing.

"Hello, excuse me, I like your music. Please, can you teach me how to make music," Mr. Squirrel says.

Koo and Moo skip far away from Mr. Squirrel and shout. "You have no wings. We make music with our wings and legs. We cannot teach you how to make music," they both say.

Mr. Squirrel skips and hops to a nearby tree.

He is sad, but not for a long time.

He starts to scratch the tree trunk with his sharp toenails.

Then, he hears the scratching make sounds.

He puts his hands together.

He also hears the claws make sounds too.

He does it again, and again and again.

He scratches the tree three times.

He puts his hands together and sings.

"Trixxxxx-nnnnn-trixxxxx! Nnnnnn-trixxxxx-nnnnn."

He hops up and down. He is happy.

Mr. Squirrel wants Koo and Moo to listen to his music.

He comes back to show Koo and Moo his music.

When Koo and Moo see Mr. Squirrel,

they skip far away from him again.

They watch him from a far-off distance.

"Here he comes again."

"He is upset with us for not teaching him how to make music,"

Koo and Moo say.

They both hop further away from Mr. Squirrel.

Mr. Squirrel is alone with no one to share his music with.

He sits at the bottom of the tree.

Afterwards, he decides to sing and be happy.

He scratches the tree three times, claps his hands.

"Trixxxxx-nnnnn-trixxxxx! Nnnnnn-trixxxxx-nnnnn-trixxxxx."

He does it again, and again and again.

He skips, and he hops up and down.

He sings along, and he is happy.

Next, comes Squirrel AB.
She sits, watching
Mr. Squirrel, as he sings.

"Hello, excuse me, I like your
music. Please, can you teach
me how to make music?"
Squirrel AB says.

Mr. Squirrel is happy Squirrel AB likes his music.

He hops up and down twice.

"Yes, I am happy to teach you how to make music,"

Mr. Squirrel says.

"If you can do what I do, we can both make good music."

"Thank you," says Squirrel AB.

"You are welcome," says Mr. Squirrel.

He scratches the tree three times and claps his hands.

Squirrel AB also scratches the tree three times and claps her hands.

"Trixxxxx-nnnnn-trixxxxx! Nnnnnn-trixxxxx-nnnnn."

They both do it again, and again and again.

Their music become louder.

Next, Squirrel CD, Squirrel EF, and Squirrel GH come to listen.

They sit, watching Squirrel AB and Mr. Squirrel sing.

"Hello, excuse us, we like your music," the three squirrels say.

"Please, can you teach us how to make music?"

Mr. Squirrel hops up and down three times.

"Yes, I am happy to teach you how to make music," he says.

"If all of you can do what I do, we can all make very good music."

"Thank you," the three squirrels say.

"You are all welcome," Mr. Squirrel says.

He scratches the tree three times and claps his hands.

The other squirrels also scratch the tree three times and clap their hands

"Trixxxxx-nnnnn-trixxxxx! Nnnnnn-trixxxxx-nnnnn."

They all do it again, and again and again.

They scratch the tree three times and clap their hands.

"Trixxxxx-nnnnn-trixxxxx! Nnnnnn-trixxxxx-nnnnn."

So, they make very good music and become a choir.

They skip, hop up and down, as they sing. They are happy.

Their music become louder and better.
Trixxxxx-nnnnn-trixxxxx!
Nnnnnn-trixxxxx-nnnnn.

Next, Koo and Moo come to listen.
They watch all the squirrels singing from a far-off distance.

Koo says to Moo, "can squirrels make music and sing too?"

"Yes, squirrels too can make music, sing, and choose to be happy,"

Moo replies.

Afterwards, they hop and skip away for supper.

They never skip their meals.